SARAH SITS SHIVA FOR HERSELF
By Reid Pope

Uproar Theatrics

LICENSING & PRODUCTION INQUIRIES
Uproar Theatrics, LLC.
hello@uproartheatrics.com | www.UproarTheatrics.com

Characters

SARAH

> 27. Dying. Slowly losing her shit but masking it
> with berserk confidence.
> White T-Shirt Red Suspenders, Jeans, Barefoot

JEANIE

> Sarah's very Jewish mother. Can't ever really sit
> still. Can't ever really stop looking at Sarah. Skirt
> and Blazer Ensemble, White Shirt Underneath,
> Sensible Shoes To Match

MO

> Sarah's ex-girlfriend. 25. Quiet with a cutting
> energy. Didn't need to show up but did. Green Rain
> Jacket, Grey Stretch Workout Pants, Sneakers,
> Helmet In Hand

LOU

> Jeanie's childhood best friend. Older, disheveled.
> Has an almost-not-quite New York accent. Dark
> Shorts, Dark T-Shirt, Blanket (on couch, but soon
> becomes a part of him)

Note For Actors/ Readers:

Lean into fast, funny bing-bang-boom dialogue. Step on
each other's lines. Let the tension escalate so that beats land
with meaning… then start the play's engine up again.
// signifies definite overlapping lines. The cadence of the rest
is up to you. It should all feel pretty natural. Well, as natural
as a preemptive shiva in a kinda conventional kinda
unconventional Jewish home can be.

SARAH SITS SHIVA FOR HERSELF
By Reid Pope

Lights up on:
Sarah. Center. Standing on a chair.
She clutches her head.
Her Hair. In two fists.

Jeanie stands SR. At rise, she drops to her knees
and lets out a blood-curdling scream.

JEANIE

NOoooooo!

Sarah lets go of her hair. Looks at the audience
as the "NO!" fades out...

SARAH

My mother never let me dye my hair.
The chlorine from my summers of swimming lightened it,
and in her opinion, "that was enough"

She was queen of rules, my mother.
No piercings til 16, and even then, just ears.
No tattoos.
No drinking.
No smoking.

No slip and slides at birthday parties because your cousin
broke his femur in a plastic swimming pool at age two and
even though a slip and slide is not a plastic swimming pool
it's close and we don't need any more broken femurs or full
body casts in this household.
No. No. No. No. No we do not.

SARAH (cont)

I wonder what it would feel like to be in a full body cast
when you're not 2. My cousin pooped himself, ate oreos, and
played legos in it.
They found all that inside when they cut it off.

He was covered in scratches.
I wonder if I'd be.
Covered in scratches or clean?

I don't think I'd move around as much inside of it. I've
gotten pretty good at staying still. Gotten pretty good at...
Staying...

Beat.

The thinking time would get to me, though. For sure.
When you're older than 2, being alone with your thoughts is
difficult.
Sometimes entertaining, but most of the time it feels like... I
dunno... stepping on a lego?

At least stepping on a lego is unpredictable. So is dying your
hair.
Dying though? Dying is predictable as hell. Everyone does
it.
It's just a question of when. And how, I suppose.

When and
How and
What you represent when you go?

What you represent when you...

*Sarah looks at us for a bit longer, then plops
down on her chair.*

As she sits, the lights shift to reveal that we are in...

A living room, mid-morning:

Three chairs and a couch arranged in a semicircle.

In the middle of the semicircle: a coffee table. On it: a chalkboard, crown, shell, photo frame, dreidel, menorah, CDs, bottle caps, and some magic cards.

LOU lounges on the couch holding a rectangular baking pan. MO sits upright and awkward in her chair. She unbuckles her helmet and places it beside her.

JEANIE rises and moves to her rightful place between Sarah and Lou.

SARAH

Welcome to my shiva. A shiva I have thrown for myself.

JEANIE

A shiva she has thrown for herself even though she is still very much alive!

SARAH

But soon to be dead!

JEANIE

But soon to be- Hey, no! Let's not talk like that.

SARAH

Why deny it? This is my shiva. A shiva I have thrown for myself. A shiva that I am having because my death is rapidly approaching, and I'm so glad all of you could be here today.

MO

Honored.

LOU

Pleasure. I brought Kugel because it was the Jewish thing to do.

JEANIE

Wonderful. Thank you, Lou. You are a great Jew.

SARAH

Yes, thank you Lou The Great Jew, and a great big FUCK YOU to the other 13 people I invited who failed to show up.

LOU

It's a weekday.

MO

And a workday.

SARAH

You're here.

MO

I'm unemployed.

LOU

I'm retired.

JEANIE (without anyone asking)

And I'm your mother!

SARAH

Still. I'm dying. More people should've

JEANIE

Sarah, honey why don't you explain what a Shiva is to your
friend here.

SARAH

She knows what a shiva is.

JEANIE (to Mo)

You know what a shiva is?

MO

Sorta.

JEANIE

Sorta is not knowing. What do I always say, Sarah? What
have I always said? Sorta is not knowing!

SARAH

Ok fine. I will explain what a Shiva is to my ex-*girlfriend*
here. And, I mean, the fact that she is here- the fact that you
are here is just- well...

LOU (abrasively shout-reading off his phone)

In Judaism a shiva is a traditional period of mourning.
Friends and family gather to remember a person's life.
You're also not supposed to shave and you're supposed to
cover the mirrors and the person is supposed to be dead, very
dead, already buried deep in the ground but this is- I guess
this shiva's a little more... unconventional.

SARAH

Yes. This is unconventional. We hate convention in this
home.

JEANIE

Well we don't hate it.

SARAH

We hate it.

JEANIE

We don't HAte it- b ... well anyway thank you Lou. For that
helpful explanation. You're always helping. You know, Lou
and I have been friends since the third grade.

SARAH

I know.

JEANIE

I know you know, I wasn't talking to you, I was talking to
your friend here.

SARAH

My ex-girlfriend. And these days we just say third grade.

JEANIE

Well these days third graders are smoking pot and having sex
so how about we stick to saying it the old way huh?

SARAH (looking at Mo and laughing a bit)

Jesus

JEANIE (to Lou, rapid-fire)

She comes to me and says... I want to have a shiva for
myself. And I say a Shiva? But those are for people who are
dead and you are very much alive. Plus we're not even that
religious. She says: I don't care I'm gonna die soon and I
want a shiva and I need to be here alive to make sure you do
it and make sure you do it *right*. And I said ok, but I think it
breaks a lot of rules, a lot of biblical laws, and she says mom
I sleep with women I have 36 tattoos I've broken a lot of

6

JEANIE (cont)
laws and I say THE JEWS HAVE NO PROBLEMS WITH
HOMOSEXUALITY plus 36 is a Jewish number.

SARAH
And I tell her The Jews actually do have problems with
homosexuality, in July of last year, Yishai Schlissel, a Jew,
waded into a Gay Pride parade in Jerusalem with a knife and
stabbed a 16-year-old girl// to death. So…

JEANIE
//And I said, where did you hear such a thing, I've never
heard of such a thing, and even if such a thing did happen,
we're not that kind of Jewish. // No we're…

LOU
// Not that kind of Jewish.

JEANIE
But then she says alright, if we're not that kind of Jewish,
what kind of Jewish are we?

Beat.

JEANIE
And with that she had me stumped. Stumped as a cut-down
giving tree.

She turns to Lou.

JEANIE
As you know, I'm very giving.

LOU (staring at the Kugel)
You give so much.

SARAH

Well, Mo. I'm sure you're enthralled by all of this.

MO

No, it's… it's fascinating. And good to be here. Good to see… you.

SARAH

Good to see me before I die.

LOU

She's so casual about it.

JEANIE

I've said it before and I'll say it again. Humor is a coping mechanism.

SARAH

Please don't say it again.

JEANIE

HUMOR IS A COPING MECHANISM!

LOU

Well if it is, she's been coping her whole life, because she's always been quite funny.

SARAH

Oh good, you've started talking about me. Recounting memories and such. Here, let me lie down and pretend to be dead. You all just keep going.

> *She lies down, dramatically sprawling out on the floor.*

SARAH

I put some stuff on the coffee table to jog your memory...
bring you back to the good old days. The crown from when I
was middle school spelling queen, my magic cards, yada
yada.

LOU

Why the menorah and dreidel? It's March.

JEANIE

Oh, those were me. I needed- she didn't have anything
Jewish. I said, you're gonna throw a Jewish event for
yourself and not have anything Jewish on display? So I
tossed em in.

LOU

Love it.

They look at Mo.

She doesn't really know what to do.

MO

I... also... love it?

JEANIE & LOU

Good.

*Mo is uncomfortable but glad her response
made them happy.*

After a moment...

MO

We played with those magic cards on that snow day, when
was it... Two years ago? Remember that dance-move you
made up? God, what was it called?

Silence.

MO

Sarah?

More silence. She taps Sarah's knee.

SARAH (opening one eye)

I'm dead so I cannot answer. But if I was alive I would remind you that it was called the Lazy Susan.

MO

Yes! The Lazy Susan! Oh man you were spinning around the living room just bonking into things saying look! Look! I made up a new dance move *where I just let people push me around and get what they want from me...* it's called the Lazy Susan! It's called the–

Mo giggles and spins. Moves her hips in a circle. Gets lost in the memory.

MO

So clever.

JEANIE

You know, you should never let people push you around.

MO

It was a joke. A- a- clever

JEANIE (throwing her arms up)

I'm just *saying.* You should never let people push you around.

SARAH (from the ground)

<u>Thank you mom for another teachable moment.</u> Any other memories about me? Questions?

LOU

I thought you were supposed to be dead.

JEANIE

Lou!

LOU

What, she said it earlier- "Here let me lie down and pretend to be dead and you all just keep talkin"

SARAH

Questionnnnnnsss ?

LOU

Well I do have a question, but I'm not sure it's appropriate//
 for the s

SARAH

//Anything and everything is appropriate! I'm an open book.
Don't want to take anything to the grave!

JEANIE

Ok but Lou has a history// of

LOU

//How do- How does it work with-With the two of you-
When you used to be intimate? The two of you? How does
that- I never understood how that works…

JEANIE (astonished)
Lou! See? What did I tell ya! He has a history// of over

Sarah pops up, howling with laughter.

SARAH

//Ohhhhhh so that's what you wanna know!?

11

MO

Sarah. No.

SARAH

What? Why not? C'mon. The man's curious.

MO

Sarah, I swear to god.

JEANIE

Don't swear to god.

MO

Ok fine! I swear to - I SWEAR ON MY MOTHERS LIFE//
if you explain lesbian sex to this man right here and now I
will kill you.

JEANIE (appalled at the mother's life bit)
// Oh! Don't swear on your mother's-

SARAH

Great. Do it before the cancer does.

JEANIE

Sarah!

SARAH

WHAT? I'm coping!

She crawls over to Mo.

SARAH

Why are you so prudish all of a sudden? The man's curious.

MO

The man also lives in Brooklyn and I live in Brooklyn. And though Brooklyn is *big* it's also very very <u>small</u> ... and if I happen to be walking around the streets of Brooklyn on a day that it is very very small, I will most likely run into Lou. And all Lou will be able to think about is our- well our- our- ... ALL LOU WILL BE ABLE TO THINK ABOUT IS LESBIAN SEX AND ALL I WILL BE ABLE TO THINK ABOUT IS LESBIAN SEX AND SOON ENOUGH THE WHOLE ENTIRE BOROUGH WILL JUST BE TALKING ABOUT THE CAREFULLY CHOREOGRAPHED LEWD LOGISTICS OF LESBIAN SEX.

> *Lou takes his fork, peels back the tin foil, and slowly begins to eat the Kugel he brought, sinking into himself.*

SARAH

That sounds like a fantastic thing to be thinking about.

MO

I'm gonna kill you.

SARAH (flirty)

If you do, do it softly.

JEANIE

Hey now girls. Let's just... either answer Lou or move on.

> *Sarah turns to look at her.*

SARAH

Oh my god. Oh my god, *you* don't know how it works either. My own MOTHER doesn't know h- Oh wow this is

MO

Sarah, don't.

13

SARAH

This is a THRILL, really. Who knew my shiva would of sex and secrets and *She looks at Mo, then takes a breath.*

SARAH

OK fine. I won't talk about it... today. But we have six more days of this. Who's to say it won't just *slip out* on day four or five?

MO

Six more days of...?

JEANIE

Shiva in Hebrew means seven. It is tradition to sit here and mourn her death for seven days. Lou forgot that in his little explanation.

MO

Oh I don't know if I'm

SARAH

Aren't you wildly unemployed?

MO

I mean yes, but I- I... Ok. But lay off the

SARAH

Alright. I'll lay off the stuff that you would have to talk about with Lou on a "small day" in Brooklyn... whatever that means.

The doorbell rings.

SARAH

Ohp! That must be the edible arrangement.

14

MO (surprised, kind of)
You ordered an edible arrangement?

SARAH & JEANIE
It's not a proper shiva without an edible arrangement.

LOU (now with a mouthful of Kugel)
They're right. Been to six shivas this year. All of them-
beautiful mountains of fruit.

Sarah bounces offstage to answer the door.

Awkward silence.

Lou chews slowly.

Jeanie studies Mo.

Finally...

JEANIE
If Sarah didn't get sick, wouldyou've married her?

MO (thrown)
What?

They look at her.

She backpedals a bit.

MO
I mean. I feel... I feel like that's an unfair- that's just not a
fair question.

LOU (mouth full)
Life isn't fair.

Jeanie and Mo ignore him.

JEANIE

Well?

MO

Well what?

JEANIE

Well give me some sort of answer because I'm her mother and she's dying and you're obviously not going to marry her now, so just give me some sort of answer.

MO

When we were together, she made my life happy and full. If she were- if she wasn't- if things were different and we were still together then my life would continue to be very happy and full.

JEANIE

That wasn't an answer.

LOU

I'm alone. Been alone my whole life and I'm always happy and most of the time full. Except after eating those little KIND bars. What kind of facacta shit is that? Little grains of rice and two chocolate chips fused together in a little rectangle

JEANIE (quickly turning to Lou)

Lou, I've told you 100 times. Kind bars are not meal replacements. They are just a snack, something to get your blood sugar back up when it has gotten low.

She turns back to Mo.

JEANIE

Ok sure, "happy and full" yeah yeah yada yada yada, but
would you've married her?

MO

I'd
I just don't think th–

Sarah comes back with a very sad looking edible
arrangement.

JEANIE

Well, would you look at that.

SARAH

It's awful.

MO

It's not awful.

SARAH

It's awful.

MO

I told you you should've spent money on a real one.

JEANIE

Whatdyou mean a real one?

MO

She got it from a discount store. Knock-off version. The real
ones were too expensive.

LOU (head cocked to one side)
Is it supposed to be dripping like that?

SARAH (sarcastically)
Yeah, it's crying. For me. I put in a special request for a
crying one. Cuz I'm dying.

JEANIE
What do you mean too expensive? She has money. We have
m

MO (too loud, frustrated)
She's been paying the hospital bills herself.

JEANIE
What.... Why would you pay the- ? ... I told you to send me
the bills, Sarah.

SARAH
I sent you some.

JEANIE
SOME!? WHY SOME!? WHY NOT ALL THE-!? SARAH I
AM YOUR MOTHER AND WE HAVE MONEY AND I
COULD'VE PAID THE- YOU HAVE NO REASON TO BE
GOING BEHIND MY BACK AND DOING THAT AND
DOING THAT YOURSELF AND PUTTING YOURSELF
IN DEBT YOU HAVE NO REASON TO BE- WHY
WOULD Y

SARAH
To take some weight off.

JEANIE
Weight? What *weight*?

SARAH

My weight, the lasting dad grief weight, the your job weight - you have a lot of weight on you and around you and with you and a hell of a lot more coming for you in the near future and I just wanted to take a little off.

Beat.

Another.

Jeanie moves to take a closer look at the discount edible arrangement.

JEANIE (teary-eyed)

Well, it's- it's beautiful.

SARAH

You don't have to lie.

JEANIE

No it's really… look, it even has 18 little strawberries around the edges. 18, a Jewish number.

SARAH

I didn't know how many people were gonna show up. I just wanted people to be fed. Turns out, I only have 3 people in my life who care about me. Well… two people and a Lou.

LOU

Hey.

MO

She's kidding.

SARAH

I'm kidding.

*Sarah puts the edible arrangement on the coffee
table in the middle. Sits.*

LOU
I know. I just dunno how you can keep your spirits so high in
the face of all this.
(to Jeanie)
No parent should have to bury their child.

JEANIE
No parent should have t

Silence.

A long dose of it.

*They sit and stare at the sad looking edible
arrangement.*

Sarah is gutted.

Jeanie sees this.

Takes a moment, then breaks the silence...

JEANIE
Well... what do we do now?
I would say a prayer, but I don't even know what's appropri

LOU
We sit.

Beat.

We sit with it all.

Beat.

LOU (cont)
With the cancer and the death and the sadness and the fruit

Beat.

The lesbian sex...

Mo cringes.

JEANIE
I've never been good at sitting.

LOU
No. No you have not. But you have 7 days to practice. 7 days to try.

JEANIE
7 days to practice. 7 days to

The lights shift.

Sarah looks out at the audience.

SARAH
When you're older than 2, being alone with your thoughts is difficult.
Sometimes entertaining, but most of the time it feels like …
I dunno… stepping on a lego?

At least stepping on a lego is unpredictable. So is dying your hair.
Dying though? Dying is predictable as hell.

Everyone does it.

It's just a question of when.
And how, I suppose.

SARAH (cont)
When and how and what you represent when you go.

What you represent when you…

After a long while…

JEANIE
Now what's that supposed to mean?

SARAH
(shocked and taken out of her private monologue moment)
W-what?

The lights shift.
We're back in the living room.

JEANIE
"Representation"… What you "represent" when you go- what
you- what you

LOU
Yeah, what's that supposed ta mean? "Represent" like what
you represenTED on earth. What you did and meant and felt
and how you touched people when you were here… or what
you- well, what you- what it symbolizes and means when
you… uh… pass on…? What *we're* left to sort of… *deal*
with once you've… you know… ?

Sarah sinks into herself.

JEANIE
Lou.

LOU
What?

22

                         JEANIE

I just

                          LOU

You brought it up first.

                         JEANIE

Don't be childish.

                          LOU

I'm not being CHILDISH I'm talking about <u>representation.</u>
That's not childish that's- it's a deep adult thing to be talking
about! No child thinks about what they- what they represent,
why they're here! Representation is a very ADULT thing.

            Mo moves closer to Sarah. Sits at her feet.

                          MO

Sare?

            Beat.

Is everything...? Are... you...?

            Sarah is unresponsive.

                    MO (grabbing her hand)

We don't have to- we don't have to talk about this. Sorry we-
sorry we overheard your whole little internal- th-thing. Sorry
we brought this up// we don't have to talk about-

                    JEANIE (under breath)

//Technically she brought it up.

            *Mo gives Jeanie a look, then turns back to
            Sarah.*

MO

Are you feeling ok? Do you want to lie down… or
something?
I can
We can go…
Leave you to your…

JEANIE (sudden, eyes locked on Sarah)

No. Nobody's going anywhere.

MO

Um ok.

JEANIE

Nobody's going anywhere. Everyone's staying right here.

LOU

It *is* getting late.

JEANIE

You were the one JUST talking about sitting with things,
sitting here and thinking and waiting and praying... well not
really praying... but you know, doing our own sort of… THE
POINT IS nobody's going anywhere. Everybody's staying
right here and that is what's happening.

LOU (defensive)

Ok.

JEANIE

You were the one just talking about how w–

LOU

Fair. You made a fair point, Jeanie. We're here. We're// not
going–

MO

Sarah?

Sarah runs her hand over the paneling of her chair. Somewhere else.

Jeanie puts a hand on Mo's shoulder.

JEANIE

Why don't you just let her be for a bit, huh?

Beat.

Mo wriggles out of Jeanie's grasp. Looks at Sarah, then backs off a little.

MO

Ok. I'm just

JEANIE

Worried. Yeah. I know.

She leans toward Sarah.

JEANIE

We all are…
Have to remind myself that there's nothing we can really- well nothing to be "worried about" really. Nothing really *worth* worrying about… Not like we can do anything. Anything to help or stop the whole… whatever. So at the end of the day, *worrying* really isn't going to- isn't really going to…

LOU (loudly reading off his phone again)
DID YOU KNOW that President Calvin Coolidge was a man
of such taciturn character and passive demeanor, that when
told that he died, the pundit H.L. Mencken replied, "how can
you tell?"

Beat.

They sit with that information.

Sarah's still tracing the furniture.

MO
"How can you tell"... rough.

JEANIE
What in the world did you look up to get that information?

LOU
How d'you know I didn't just know it off the top of my
head?

JEANIE
Because you used the word "pundit"

LOU
I could know the word "pundit"

JEANIE
You *could've*. Sure. But I don't think you did before you

Lou cracks.

LOU
Fine. I put "what you represent when you go" into The
phone Safari.

JEANIE

I knew it. Also you're not supposed to use The Safari anymore, Lou. You're supposed to use The Chrome.

Turning to Mo.

JEANIE

Isn't that right, Mo? You're supposed to use the Chrome? Sarah was telling me just the other day that it's best to use The

MO (still studying at Sarah, concerned)

Uh... yeah Chrome is better but either search thing works.

JEANIE

Good to know.

LOU

I don't have the Chrome on my phone. Just the Safari.

MO (disinterested)

Either one works.

Beat.

Another.

LOU

I sure hope people don't say that about me.

JEANIE

Say what about you?

LOU

"How can you tell"... when I die... I don't want pundit HL Mencken or you or the folks from the synagogue to make jokes about how "I never lived" and stuff.

JEANIE

Lou, we would never make

LOU

I just worry. You know. I don't have much- don't *represent*
much in this
Like I said before, I'm alone and I'm fine.
Fine with- I'm full and happy and fulfilled mostly …fulfilled
and happy…

JEANIE

Then you're fine!

LOU

But I don't... th- thank you, I know I'm fine, and I'm fine
with being... *fine*... but I just don't know if I'm fine with not
representing something.

JEANIE

All this representing talk, I still don't know what it even
means. We are all here. All living. Breathing. Moving.
Talking. We are people. Not representations of people. No.
Not representations. We are all living, breathing, people.
Real. People. Here. and ALIVE.

MO

I think Sarah just meant, what do you- like… like- what you
leave behind? What sort of "dent" did you make in the
world? While you were on the planet? And- And how?
…
Did it matter? Did *you* matter?

                    JEANIE
Well of course she mattered!
Matters.
She's still here.
Mattering.
Mattering right here!

                    LOU

Yes.

                    MO

Of course.
I just meant- I think she just meant

          JEANIE (unintentionally cutting)
Let's not put words in her mouth.

                    MO

I'M NOT
I'M NOT PUTTING WORDS IN HER MOUTH, JEANIE,
SHE'S JUST NOT TALKING! WE WE HAD
CONVERSATIONS ABOUT THIS. ABOUT ALL OF THIS.
ABOUT LIVING AND BREATHING AND DYING AND
DENTS. ABOUT MAKING A DIFFERENCE AND
WHETHER YOU CAN GO ON CARING ABOUT
SOMEONE, LOV… ING SOMEONE AFTER YOU-
AFTER SOMEONE- AFTER- AFTER- ABOUT WHAT
LASTS AND WHAT *CAN* LAST AND WHAT *SHOULD*
LAST AND…. ALL OF IT.

          She takes a breath. Lowers her voice a bit.

MO
We'd sit in that hospital room and she'd eat that shitty mushroom soup and I'd look at her face and the bags under her eyes and her skin and her stupid, STUPID smile despite it all, and we'd talk about it. Did you not think we- who do you think w
What do you think we meant to one another?

Beat.

Another.

Jeanie and Mo stare at one another.

For a long time.

Suddenly:

SARAH (monotone)
I want to dye my hair.

MO
What?

SARAH (still numb, monotone, staring straight ahead)
I want to dye my hair. Right now.

JEANIE
Honey, I

LOU
Are you sure that's a

SARAH
I want to dye my hair right now I want to dye my hair at my shiva I want to feel something I want to dye my hair.

MO

Ok.

JEANIE

Mo, I

MO (with increased confidence)
Ok. Yes.
YES. Let's do it.
We're doing this!

LOU

I

MO (jumping up, gesturing to Jeanie and Lou)
You heard the woman!
She wants to dye her hair!
We're gonna dye her hair!
We're gonna dye her hair, god dammit!

Jeanie flinches at the profanity.

Sarah doesn't move.

MO

Everybody up!

Lou and Jeanie stand reluctantly.

MO

Jeanie, you have gloves?

JEANIE

Under the sink.

MO

Great. You're on glove duty. Lou, go get a towel to throw over the carpet. I'm going to the pharmacy on 3rd. They should have some sort of dye-

JEANIE

Some sort of dye! Oy, Sarah are you sure you want to

Sarah has not moved.

SARAH

I want to feel something.

Beat.

JEANIE

Ok.

MO (looking at her)

She wants to feel something.

LOU

She wants to feel something!

SARAH

I want to do something. Feel something. Do something before I die. I want to dye my hair. I want to *do something, have...* something...

The lights flicker... shift.

Jeanie looks at Sarah.
Mo and Lou freeze.

JEANIE
She used to come into our room at night.
3am like clockwork.
For a month or so.
When she was six.

Say…
Mom.
Dad.

I don't want to die.
I don't want to be buried in the ground.
I don't want to explode with the earth when the earth
explodes.

I don't want to die.

She'd have this recurring dream.
Where her gravestone would shatter to pieces.
Shatter to pieces as the earth did.

She'd see herself being hurtled into space, I guess?
Hurtled into space away from earth and into oblivion.

Visualize her little body spinning into oblivion.

Well she didn't use the word oblivion.
She was six.

But the sentiment
Was.
The sentiment was there.

She was scared of that sorta sentiment

And Ben would try to tackle it.
The question of where you go when you die

JEANIE (cont)
After you die.

3am her dad and her mom
trying to explain what happens when

What do you tell a six year old when she's shaking at the
foot of your bed? Sobbing and begging you to tell her that
she's not gonna die.
That it's not gonna happen?
That she's not going to turn to dust?

What do you... ?

We'd change up the answer.
Week in and week out.

Ben'd tell her some mythical tale of the sky.

Heaven-like.

After...

Life.

Beyond?

He was good at telling stories like that.

He'd hold her and sing a little song.
Something he made up on the spot.
About life and doing good and making the most of your time
on earth. Making the most of your time here before you go
up. Something like that.

It would work, sometimes.

JEANIE (cont)
She'd calm down.

Breathing would go back to normal.

And she'd go back to bed.
Or pass out at the foot of ours and we'd carry her down the
hall.

She'd sleep til morning.

Other times, she'd come back an hour or two later.

Crying. Again.

A new vision of her little body hurtling through space.
Spinning out into...

...

...

What are you supposed to say, huh?
At 3am when your 6 year old kid is crying about death?

...

What about when she's 26 and not crying at all?

26 and not crying at all just...

...

Just sitting there.

...

Gesturing to a still-frozen Sarah.

JEANIE (cont)
One minute bouncing off the walls
and the next

Just…

Gesturing.

Lights up on: the same room. 30 minutes later.

*Sarah sits on the floor (center) in front of the
coffee table.*
A towel beneath her. Another on her head.

*Lou's on the couch. Jeanie takes her spot beside
him.*

*Mo crouches down next to Sarah– a handheld
mirror in her left hand, phone in the other.*

MO
Alright. You can

*She gestures to the towel on Sarah's head. Sarah
reaches up and removes it.*

Jeanie flinches.
Lou stares.

Her hair is blue. Very blue.

Mo hands her the mirror.

MO
Do you like it?

SARAH (monotone)

I love it.

LOU

Doesn't seem like you like it.

SARAH (still monotone)
I don't like it. I love it.

JEANIE

The jokes are back.

LOU
Does it count as a joke if it's said like that?

MO

Said like what?

LOU
In that tone of voice... or... well... more like... with an
absence of any sort of...

SARAH (monotone)

Life?

JEANIE

Sarah. Come on.

LOU
Why is she- at the beginning of this she was all silly and
peppy and WELCOME TO MY SHIVA SHIVA I HAVE
THROWN FOR MYSELF WOO and now she's all... even
after the hair and the blue and the big styling to-do she's
all...

MO

Oh I don't know Lou, maybe because she's dying?

LOU

She was dying before.

JEANIE

Hey.

LOU

What? She was. Nothing has. Not much has changed. Has it?

Beat.

LOU

I mean, did something? Did something change?

JEANIE

No nothing... nothing ch- nothing *has* to change for you to- well for you to

She looks at Sarah.

JEANIE

Can't believe I have a kid with blue hair.

She laughs.

JEANIE

What kind of Jewish mother am I? Letting my daughter dye her hair? Letting my daughter dye her hair blue?

MO

Well blue is a Jewish color, is it not?

Lou and Jeanie look at her.

MO

What? Am I wrong?

JEANIE

No you're not wrong.

LOU

Not wrong.

JEANIE

It's just... having a kid with dyed hair, letting her dye her hair, especially blue, if she were- if she were in high school or college or out in the open and not in this living room- people would... well people would talk...

LOU

People would definitely talk.

MO

So blue represents something?

JEANIE

What?

MO

The blue, the hair dye, people would talk about it because it represents something. Something different. Something... alien.

JEANIE

Well not *alien*. But... different, sure. Unconventional.

LOU

Jews always have guilt about convention. Well being unconventional. A whole history of-

MO

Makes sense.

LOU

So you pile blue hair and hair dye and your kid dying onto
 that history and it all gets a little...

JEANIE

Heavy.

Sarah looks at Jeanie.

JEANIE

It a little... heavy. Yeah.

SARAH

You don't like the blue.

JEANIE

It's fine. If it makes you happy it's

SARAH

You like the blue, Lou?

LOU

If it makes you happy.

SARAH

Mo?

Mo looks at her.

MO

You know how I feel about

Beat.

*She studies her hair. Then her eyes. Then back to
the hair.*

MO

I figured that's why you picked the
Is it selfish to think that you picked it because of…

The lights shift.

*Mo stands. Takes the handheld mirror from
Sarah and studies herself.*

*The stage is tinted now… dark. Navy. Everyone
except Mo fades. Freezes.*

MO

Sarah and I were Joni Mitchell fans. Yeah, I know…
predictable. The most lesbian thing. Got burnt out after a
while. You can only listen to folk for so long
The crooning is soothing or whatever, sure… but also creates
a sort of chasm? A pit deep in your gut.

*She hums a bit of something that sounds like
Joni Mitchell's Blue.*

Blue– was one of our favorites. The album and the song.

We listened to the thing on a loop in the hospital.

Her mom couldn't always make it to the chemo sessions and
it reminded her of- home? I guess… Something.

Felt strange to sit there and listen. Like I was invading her
childhood memories or something. Felt wrong to fall in love
with the song because it wasn't mine?

It was ours, sure. But it wasn't

MO (cont)
Anyway, she'd lie there and I'd hold her hand and we'd hum
along. Humming was safe. Safe for us and cuz I didn't
know...cuz I still don't really know all the words. Like I
said, I still fuck up the- order of... [things]

*She hums a bit of something that sounds like
Joni Mitchell's Blue.*

For a good while.

As the lights shift.

*Mo crouches down and holds the mirror up so
Sarah can look at her hair again.*

MO
Is it crazy that I thought-?

Sarah turns to look at Mo.

Kisses her.

It's sudden but slow.

JEANIE (thrown)
Woahoho-ok.

Lou pulls his blanket up.

Sarah turns to look at them both.

And very slowly...

Begins to laugh.

SARAH

Still can't deal with it, can you?

MO

Sarah...

SARAH

What? No. Don't pretend you didn't hear her little inhale-
the reaction.

JEANIE

Sarah, c'mon- I've been so supportive of your- of this
whole- it's just that- you *broke up*. That's all. Right? You two
aren't together anymore and this whole thing has just been-
very

LOU

A lot. This whole thing has just been *a lot* for... your mother.
For everyone, I can imagine.

SARAH

Very a lot
Very a lot
Nice.
Sure
Look it's fine.
It's fine if you cringed cuz of the kiss.
I just want you to- like. Just admit it.

　　　Beat.

I still cringe sometimes when I see- when I watch other-
when I watch other... happy people? In public? Other happy
people like us... together... showing affection... or
whatever... I still do it... it's just

MO

Internalized homophobia.

SARAH

Sure. Yeah. But I admit it. Acknowledge it. Recognize my
own discomfort. If you admit it and recognize it, it's less
fucked up.

JEANIE

Is it? //Also enough with the cursing Sarah, it's

MO

//Used to joke that I wanted a reboot of *Friends*. Just me and
my internalized homophobia hanging out. Cuz we're such
close pals.

Sarah and Lou laugh.

SARAH

That's pretty good, Mo.

MO (proud)

You're not the only comedian here, Sarah Lynn.

LOU (to Jeanie)

I forgot you named her that. After Ben's sister.

JEANIE

Yeah. Figured she'd… thought she'd carry on Lynne's
legacy once Lynn… // well now it's sort of … a way to
honor him too I guess…

SARAH
(back to trying to distract from the heaviness)
It's so interesting what's still programmed inside my- like
the structured programming still embedded in my brain or
whatever? The other day I was walking to the supermarket.
Walking to the supermarket by myself, and was like "huh,
I'm out here alone. All by myself. Out by myself, maybe I'll
meet a nice boy. A cute boy at Trader Joes."

MO
What?

JEANIE
What?

LOU
What?

SARAH
Yeah. My reaction exactly. It's like sometimes the societal
programming is so deeply embedded that I forget I'm... I
dunno. It happens. You get fed phrases forever, "oh, you're
going to a party? Maybe you'll meet a nice Jewish boy" "a
girl like yourself, walking around with a face like that,
you're sure to meet a nice Jewish boy at the store... at the
park... at school... at work... don't know how the boys
don't just go crazy for you, Sarah... I mean look at you!
Look at you!"

She gestures to her head.

SARAH
All plays in there on a loop. I guess. Still. Bits and pieces
still tucked into the brain cavities or whatever.

LOU
Brain cavities of whatever. Huh.

                              JEANIE
Huh.

         Beat.

         Sarah spins around.

                              SARAH
You ever seen *Friends*, Lou?

                              LOU
Oh yeah. At least like… 10 episodes. Probably. Maybe.

                              SARAH
Mo's a big fan. Thinks it's a fun nothing narrative.

                              LOU
Nothing narrative?

                              MO
Sometimes you just want to sit down and watch nothing.

                              SARAH
The show is structured around the fact that nothing TOO
crazy happens. Like Seinfeld. People find respite and
relaxation in watching nonsense and nothingness unfold… A
New York nothing narrative.

                              LOU
New York nothing narrative. Say that ten times fast.

         Mo laughs.

                      LOU (under his breath)
New York nothing narrative… New York nothing

JEANIE

That doesn't make any sense. New York nothing- there's
always something happening in New York. Always
something happening here. So that actually makes zero

SARAH

You think dad would've put up with all this?

Beat.

JEANIE

What do you mean?

SARAH

You think dad would've put up with me throwing myself a
shiva?

JEANIE

I…

SARAH

With me throwing myself a shiva and making out with my
ex-girlfriend at the shiva, dying my hair blue. Dying. In
general. You think he would've been able to sit here? Put up
with it? Deal?

JEANIE

Well he wouldn't have had much of a choice.

SARAH

What's the supposed to

JEANIE

I would've…

SARAH

You would've forced him to be here. Sit through it.

JEANIE

N-no not *force*. There wouldn't be any *forcing*, Sarah. Your father loved you. He would've attended on his own accord.

SARAH

Attended on his own accord. That sounds very organic and normal and fatherly.

JEANIE

Your father was busy and stubborn and anxious but he loved you. Busy and stubborn and anxious but he

SARAH

I don't know if he would've.

JEANIE

He would've.

SARAH

I don't know. On his own accord I don't know.

JEANIE

Sarah he would've!

SARAH

I don't know, mom.

JEANIE

Sarah!

SARAH

Mom!

JEANIE

SARAH!

                         SARAH

MOOOoooooOOmmm!!!!!!!!!!

                          MO

JESUS CHRIST.

                          LOU

Ay. Don't- at least use Moses's name in vain!

                          MO

Fine. MOSES CHRIST !!!!

                        SARAH

What?

                          MO

How long do you two usually let this go on f- I mean I've
seen it before, heard bits and pieces of the sort of thing over
the phone in the past but JESUS- Moses- CHRIST this is so
painful to sit through. Why must you push each other's
buttons? Why must ALL the buttons be CONSTANTLY
pushed?

                          LOU

The stubbornness. Her father's stubbornness. It's in the
 genes. Inherited.

                        SARAH

No I got the anxiety from my father. Neuroticism from my
mother. The stubbornness from them both. Thank you
parents. Thank you alive mom and dead dad.

                          MO

Sarah. C'mon.

JEANIE

It's fine. Let her spew whatever she wants to spew. I'm
exhausted. Plus, at this point, with all the toxins and dye
seeping into her scalp, it's probably just the chemicals
talking.

SARAH

Yes this is the blue talking. All the blue.
I'm not myself anymore, just a big blue loon.

Mo smiles.

LOU

The jokes are back. A real jokester. Just like that Joey on
Friends.

SARAH

We get it, Lou, you've seen *Friends*! 10 episodes of it! (to
Mo) next thing you know he's gonna whip out a guitar and
start playing the theme song.

They all let out a little laugh.

Quiet.

Beat.

Another.

*Sarah goes back to tracing the paneling of her
chair.*

*Jeanie has a staring contest with the edible
arrangement.*

Mo sniffs.

LOU (phone-reading, quieter now)
Jack Daniel's last words were, "one last drink please"

JEANIE

Really?

LOU

Says it right here.

JEANIE

Huh.

LOU
Dimaggio said, "I'll finally get to see Marilyn"

JEANIE (watching Sarah)
That's nice.

Sarah's somewhere else.

LOU
Mozart said, "I feel something that is not of this earth"

JEANIE

Huh.

MO
Beethoven said, "applaud, my friends, the comedy is
 finished"

LOU

Ha! Really?

MO

Yeah.

JEANIE
But he was a musician.

LOU

So.

JEANIE

A musician not a comedian. His work was beautiful not
funny.

LOU

Buh Buh Buh Buh!!! I dunno. That's pretty funny. Pretty
dramatic at least.

MO

Guess he saw humor in... by his mid-20's he was basically
deaf so.... guess he saw humor in.

SARAH

Deteriorating.

They look at her.

MO

In his hearing deteriorating. Sure.

JEANIE

My last words...
My last words are gonna be: "thank you"

Quiet.

SARAH

Are you kidding?

MO

Sarah.

LOU

I don't think she's kidding.

JEANIE

No.
I'm not
No.
My last words are going to be Thank You.
What's the problem// with thank

SARAH

//Are you freaking kidding me, mom? THANK YOU?

MO

Sarah.

SARAH

Who the HELL are you thanking? And WHAT are you
thanking them for? Thank you GOD? Thank you for killing
ME? Thank you for the life I had even though you took my
husband and daughter and left me very much alone? Thank
you for literally taking away anything and everything that
matters to me? THANK YOU? THANK YOU TO WHO?

JEANIE (quietly)

To whom.

SARAH

I AM DYING I DO NOT GIVE A SHIT ABOUT
GRAMMAR WHAT'S AN INCORRECT WHO/WHOM
GONNA DO... HUH?... KILL ME?

Quiet.

JEANIE

My last words are going to be "thank you"

LOU

I think those are good Jeanie. A good choice.

JEANIE

Thank you for giving me a job and a family and a daughter
who never took no for a- well… who- who flew in the face
of everything- *flies* in the face of everything

SARAH (soft)

Yeah *flies*. Not dead yet.

LOU

Not dead yet.

JEANIE

Thank you for a Lou who brings Kugel and reads off his
phone and tells me what people are saying about me at the
synagogue when I can't go.

She looks at Mo.

JEANIE

And thanks to the other people who I get to sit with and
make me think about things and who make my daughter
happy and to everyone in my life who has worked to help….
Take some weight off.

Beat.

She turns to Sarah.

JEANIE

Even if taking that bit of weight off involved an incredibly
stupid decision to pay- to go into debt and pay hospital bills
and do things without my

Quiet.

JEANIE
Thank you.

Sarah is crying.

Mo runs a hand through her hair.

JEANIE
Thank you.

LOU
You're welcome.

Mo looks at him.

LOU
And uh… I mean… thank you.

Beat.

LOU
Too.

Beat.

LOU
Is the hair dry yet? Can I touch it?

MO
It's dry but I don't think

SARAH
No it's… it's fine.
He can touch it. Sure.

*Lou leans forward. Puts the blanket and kugel
pan on the coffee table.*

Pokes the top of her head.

Looks at his hand.

Pokes her hair again.

LOU

Yeh, feels like hair.
Don't know what I expected.

Sarah smiles.

SARAH

Alien hair? Worms?

LOU

I dunno!

*Sarah reaches up and clenches it in her fists.
Mirroring the opening.
Tosses her head around.*

SARAH

Chemicals didn't kill it // Didn't change anything.

JEANIE

//Thank god.

SARAH

Same feeling. Same me.

LOU
But blue.

SARAH

Blue-er. Sure.

Beat.

SARAH

Blue-er... sure.
But same me.

The lights shift.

Sarah stands.
Moves forward.

Sits on the edge of the stage.

SARAH

Above all I'm just curious about what it will feel like.

Deteriorating.
Breaking down.
The slow devolve.

Cancer's confusing because technically you're filling up?
Building blocks are multiplying and spreading. Splitting and
stuffing you until you shut down...

Or whatever.

A lot of *contradictory movement*.

...

The movement isn't what scares me though.
It's more the thought of people handling me. I guess.

SARAH (cont)

Having to touch and wrap and carry my lifeless body once all my movement and bullshit has stopped.

Still.

Immobile.

Could you imagine?

Having to

Having to handle…

Lift…

Having to hold someone who has…

…

It's just fucking insane.

…

And I can see it,

The funeral.

The rabbi standing over my body.

Cuz even though I don't really want a rabbi there, you know mom's gonna get a rabbi.

The coffin will be closed and stuff.
Jews don't fuck with open casket.
We've got enough anxiety as it is.
Don't need to see death– our worst fear– realized.

No. We don't need any of that.

…

Is death our worst fear?

I mean we've dealt with a lot of death… faced a lot of death in our time… our history… or whatever…

Guess exposure therapy isn't really a thing when it comes to the fear of dying… …

Anyway

I can see the rabbi looking down at me.

Me in that box.

A little tuft of my blue hair sticking out.

My mom crying
And Lou with her.

Thank god for Lou thank god for Lou let me say it again thank god for Lou.
Thank god for…

…

They'll all be praying. And shaking their heads.

And I'll be there just overactive cells and failed organs and blue hair follicles. Still me but blue-er.

Colder.

SARAH (cont)

Hair follicles and pigment and cancer cells.

Medical stuff and medical bills and–

I just hope I made a dent.

…

Not like the kind of dent I made in the mailbox when I was 16 and learning to drive and dad distracted me by turning on the radio even though mom told him literally to never turn on the radio when I was behind the wheel.

No.

We fixed that.

That was a fix-able dent.

Not a real

I hope I made a real…

A real nasty deep heavy punch in the stomach hole in the wall shattered window BOOM BANG dent in someone's life.

In multiple people's?

Maybe that's asking for too much.
Wishful thinking. Narcissism. I dunno.

Navel gazing.

That's mom's favorite phrase to use.

SARAH (cont)
Surprised she hasn't used it yet today…

She pretends to read off her phone a-la Lou.
Mimics his voice…

Navel Gazing: Self-indulgent or excessive contemplation of oneself or a single issue, at the expense of a wider view.

A wider view.

What she asked for at the hospital, my mom.

"A room with a wider view, a better view, a view of ANYTHING other than parking lot for goodness sake, she's got CANCER she deserves to look at the river… a tree or two at bare minimum"

So they switched me.

Pushed me in that bed down the hall to a new space.

Hope that'll be exactly what this all feels like. Just a short little push.
Wheeled out of here. Onto the next adventure.

But I dunno.

Don't think so.

I think it's gonna be slow and weird and I'll lose autonomy. Someone will lift me and dress me and the rabbi will look down at the little blue tuft of my hair sticking out of the death box I'm in and he'll say some prayers even though I don't want a religious funeral that's why I had the whole- that's why I did the preemptive shiva.
The shiva was enough.

Is enough…

It has all been… enough…

I hope.

For me at least.

And for her…

….

I just think of people handling me.
Handling me like I'm a box of strawberries gone bad.

A little box of strawberries gone bad.

They'll take me and put me in the earth.

And I'll sink in.

Break apart like those little fucking legos they found buried
in my cousin's body cast. Anatomical.

Little lego pieces.

Mixed with oreos.

And dirt.

And shit.

…

And my mom will cry.

SARAH (cont)

Fill up with a sort of empty echo depression.

Swollen and hollow.

Contradictory movement.

And Mo will...

I don't know.

Watch *Friends*.

Watch *Friends* and think of nothing and enjoy thinking of nothing even though there will always be something happening... something happening something there maybe... something tucked into her brain cavity... embedded in the lining of her...

She'll watch *Friends* and think of me maybe or maybe she won't.

...

Navel gazing.

What I'm doing, right?

Thinking and hoping... desperate to have some sort of lasting influence? To be preserved in the little cavities of their...

Played on a loop.

Preserved and played on a loop in their brains.

>   *Beat.*

SARAH (cont)
And her last words … she wants them to be "thank you"

Not even about her.

A wider view.

"Thank You"

"Thank You"

God damn.

> *The lights shift.*

> *Lou gets up. Moves toward a speaker on the downstage table. Plugs his phone in.*

MO
Oh here we go. You called it. Knew that sooner or later he'd get around to playing a bad acoustic cover of the *Friends* theme

LOU (distracted, trying to plug in his phone)
Not *Friends*.

MO
Well gee, Lou, I thought we were just starting to consider each other pals! If not friends *at least* good acquaintances.

LOU
Funny. She's funny too.

SARAH
(tired, but making a valiant effort at a couple last jokes)
Yes, women are funny, Lou.

LOU (still struggling with the chord)
OKAY that's not what I meant- you know what wasn't what
I-THIS IS NOT SUPPOSED TO BE FUNNY. THIS IS
SUPPOSED TO BE

JEANIE
Just play the song Lou.

SARAH
Yeah Lou I mean you got up and walked over, most
movement I've seen from ya in a while-

JEANIE
True, more movement I've seen from ya in a long

He ignores them. Reaches down. Presses play.

*Something groovy a la "Let's Groove" by Earth
Wind & Fire begins.*

MO
Ummm.

SARAH
This song?

MO
At a shiva?

SARAH
First mom goes off on her "thank you for killing my loved
ones" spiel and now Lou wants to "groove"?

LOU
Ay! No! This isn't- I'm not grooving because of your death-
you were the one saying before it's a shiva you threw for
yourself because

JEANIE
You are still very much alive!

She gets up.

JEANIE
We are ALL. STILL. VERY MUCH. ALIVE.

Beat.

She reaches out. Takes Mo's hand. Mo stands.
They begin to dance.

Sarah watches and shakes her head.

Mo bends down. Crinkles her nose. Kisses her.
Pulls her up.

Lou begins to bop and twist in his corner.

The music plays. And plays...

They're all up and dancing now...
... moving and shaking and twirling and hurtling
around the living room.

Hurtling through space.

Lou and Jeanie shout-sing along to song.

Sarah and Mo slow-dance.

Sarah takes her crown and puts it on Mo's head.

They laugh.

66

All of them.

They laugh

and dance

and laugh

and dance

and laugh until they cry.

                              End of play.